MAX WHITLOCK

Beyond the Gold The Inspiring

Journey of Britain's Gymnastics

Legend

Michael B. Tate

TABLE OF CONTENTS

INTRODUCTION

In the world of gymnastics, where each move showcases power, accuracy, and creativity, Max Whitlock is more than just a gymnast; he is an icon. In Britain, where he has set new standards for gymnastics, his name has become practically synonymous with greatness. The documentary "Max Whitlock: Beyond the Gold - The Inspiring Journey of Britain's Gymnastics Legend" seeks to paint a nuanced and in-depth portrait of Whitlock's life and career in an effort to fully grasp the magnitude of his influence on the sport.

An incredible tale of determination, talent, and achievement is Max Whitlock's rise to gymnastics stardom. Beginning with his humble beginnings, he has gone on to accomplish a great deal, elevating not only his own career but also the sport as a whole. His unwavering commitment and groundbreaking ideas have revolutionized gymnastics, raising the bar for all competitors and motivating young athletes globally. By delving into how Whitlock's singular perspective on the sport altered expectations and perceptions, this biography aims to convey the core of his impact.

There are two goals in writing this biography. Its primary objective is to examine Whitlock's influence on gymnastics in detail. This necessitates comprehending the wider ramifications of his contributions as well as simply recounting his accomplishments. Learn all about Whitlock's impact on the sport by delving into his training routine, techniques, and competitive results. His impact as a role model in gymnastics and beyond is something the book will discuss, showing how the success of one person can motivate others and propel change.

Second, the goal of this biography is to provide more than just facts and praise. The story will delve into the personal experiences of Whitlock, illuminating his triumphs and tribulations along the way. A comprehensive portrait of Max Whitlock is sought to be painted in this biography by incorporating aspects of his childhood, professional life, and lasting impact. It will explore his driving forces, the people who have helped him along the way, and the wider influence his accomplishments will have on generations to come.

In addition to being a story of individual triumph, Max Whitlock's story reflects the larger development of gymnastics as a sport. An in-depth biography of a man who changed the game he loves and became an icon in the process is what this book claims to be. By delving into this topic, readers will gain a better understanding of Whitlock's profound influence and how his story is still shaping gymnastics today.

Max Whitlock's life is an inspiring tale of great accomplishment. A thorough reflection on his journey, accomplishments, and the legacy he is creating for future generations, "Max Whitlock: Beyond the Gold - The Inspiring Journey of Britain's Gymnastics Legend" captures the essence of his extraordinary career. Whitlock's rise from promising young gymnast to world-renowned champion is a reflection of his extraordinary talent and unfaltering commitment. The highlights of his career, which include multiple Olympic gold medals and world championships, are more than just records; they are turning points in a story of determination and innovation. The story of each accomplishment is one of relentless practice, dogged persistence, and the quest for greatness.

Looking back, Whitlock's influence on gymnastics goes well beyond his individual achievements. New benchmarks have been set by his training philosophy, technical innovations, and dedication to expanding the sport's boundaries. Not only do his own performances reflect his impact, but so do the increasingly high standards of gymnastics around the world.

Aspiration and perseverance are lessons that future generations can learn from Whitlock's story. Young athletes can find inspiration in his story, which shows that extraordinary things are possible with perseverance and commitment. The significance of aiming high, persevering through adversity, and never stopping to improve is emphasized by his legacy.

Max Whitlock's impact on the sport will be felt long after his playing days are over, and not only in terms of the hardware he won. By setting the path for subsequent gymnastics champions and shaping the sport's trajectory, his accomplishments have permanently altered the sport's trajectory.

Finally, Max Whitlock's story is an uplifting and motivating account of achievement. What he has accomplished so far is a testament to the power of passion and determination. In addition to learning about his professional life, readers are encouraged to internalize the larger message of achieving one's full potential, persevering through adversity, and making a positive difference in the world. His life and work demonstrate that greatness is within reach and can have a profound impact on those who seek to make a difference.

CHAPTER 1: EARLY LIFE

Max Whitlock's rise to gymnastic superstardom predated his appearance on the Olympic podium by many years. A mix of supportive family, natural inquisitiveness, and a fortunate introduction to gymnastics paved the way for his extraordinary career in his formative years. Gaining insight into these formative years puts his subsequent accomplishments in a profoundly human perspective.

The English town of Hemel Hempstead is the site of Max Whitlock's birth on January 13, 1993. Brian and Madeleine Whitlock gave him the kind of loving home he needed to develop his abilities. The value of perseverance and commitment was stressed by both Brian, a builder, and Madeleine, an educator. Both Max's personal and athletic development would be greatly aided by their unwavering support.

Max was a lively and inquisitive youngster who lived in Hemel Hempstead. His innate desire to be active was evident at a young age; he would frequently be seen playing sports, climbing trees, or jogging around the garden. His natural ability to move and coordinate was a precursor to the mastery that would characterize his gymnastics career. Realizing the significance of exercise for his growth, his parents actively supported his active lifestyle.

Similarly, Max grew up in a very close-knit family. Megan, his sister, was an influential figure in his formative years, and the two of them had a close relationship. The siblings developed a strong sense of camaraderie and mutual aid through their frequent participation in one another's pursuits. Because of his family dynamic, Max learned to tackle problems head-on and keep his composure under intense athletic pressure.

A fortunate turn of events brought gymnastics into Max's life. Max attended a gymnastics club birthday party when he was seven years old. Here he had his first experience with the sport that would later consume him. Max was enthralled by the gymnasts' ability to combine strength, agility, and artistry in their routines. He felt inspired to give gymnastics a go after that, and the experience stuck with him.

Max was enrolled in the Sapphire School of Gymnastics in Hemel Hempstead by his parents, who noticed his interest. With this choice, he started his official training for the sport. Coach Sam James helped Max hone his abilities, and the young man soon became known for his exceptional work ethic and innate talent. During this formative period, Max's technical knowledge and encouragement from Coach James were vital in laying a solid groundwork for his future gymnastics success.

In the first few years of training, we had both structured practice and plenty of encouragement from our instructors. Max showed an impressive aptitude for learning new skills and a determination to put in the time and effort needed to become better. It didn't take long for him to begin competing in regional and local events, as his improvement was clear. The mental fortitude and competitive drive that would characterize Max's career were shaped by these early experiences in competition.

Though gymnastics took center stage in Max's life, his parents made sure he kept a healthy perspective. They pushed Max to balance his academic and athletic pursuits, stressing the significance of education. Max gained a well-rounded perspective, an appreciation for discipline, and the ability to manage his time well through his participation in both gymnastics and academics.

It became more and more clear that Max had potential as he kept training and competing. He was able to train with some of the top in the field after his impressive performances caught the eye of more seasoned coaches. When Max was fourteen years old in 2007, he took a significant step by enrolling in the South Essex Gymnastics Club to train with Scott Hann. Because of the invaluable influence that Scott Hann's knowledge and guidance would have on Max's future competitive career, this change represented a major milestone in his growth.

Respect and a common goal-setting foundation formed the basis of Max's relationship with his coach, Scott Hann. Scott saw promise in Max and vowed to guide him to success. A great deal of dedication and self-control were required to complete the rigorous training program at South Essex Gymnastics Club. As a result of his intense interest in and commitment to the sport, Max flourished in this setting.

During these crucial years, Max's family was there for him every step of the way. When he competed, they were there to cheer him on, share in his triumphs, and console him when he lost. Max relied on this steadfast network of people to help him through the highs and lows of gymnastics competition. It jogged his memory of the lessons his parents had taught him about grit and determination when he was a little boy.

Max's early training experiences and introduction to gymnastics set the stage for his later achievements. The ideal circumstances for his success were provided by a mix of his innate abilities, committed coaching, and a loving family. He went from being an inquisitive kid at a friend's birthday party to a promising young gymnast thanks to his relentless training and unfaltering love of the sport.

During his formative years, Max also discovered how much he loved gymnastics. He reveled in the challenge of learning new routines and techniques and was enchanted by the sport's graceful precision. His enthusiasm for training and his drive to become better were clear manifestations of this drive. This passion for gymnastics laid the groundwork for his subsequent extraordinary accomplishments by propelling him to overcome challenges and test his limits.

In conclusion, Max Whitlock's early life is an account of being encouraged by family, being inquisitive as a child, and being introduced to gymnastics by chance. His talents flourished in the nurturing environment provided by his parents, Brian and Madeleine. One of the most influential factors in Max's resilience and approach to adversity was the supportive and encouraging dynamic within his close-knit family.

Max's journey in gymnastics began with his introduction to the sport when he was seven years old. His early coaches' encouragement and instruction, along with his innate ability and commitment, laid a solid groundwork for his gymnastics career. The transition to South Essex Gymnastics Club and his mentorship by Scott Hann were formative experiences; they provided the technical guidance and challenging training environment he needed to flourish as a gymnast.

The principles of tenacity and resilience that would later define Max's profession were instilled in him by his family, who were a rock during these formative years. He would go on to accomplish incredible things because his passion for gymnastics and will to win propelled him to overcome challenges and test his limits. Gaining insight into Max Whitlock's formative years puts his subsequent achievements in a human perspective, illuminating the significance of family, passion, and commitment to his path.

CHAPTER 2: JUNIOR CAREER

A tribute to Max Whitlock's early talent, perseverance, and strong support system, his journey through his junior gymnastics career is an inspiring story. Max has an incredible story of dedication and success, beginning with his first competitive steps and continuing through his transition into senior-level gymnastics. In a detailed and humanized narrative, let us delve into this crucial phase of his life.

Max had a natural talent for gymnastics and was very enthusiastic when he first started competing. Max was an outstanding gymnast who stood out at the Sapphire School of Gymnastics in Hemel Hempstead when he was a young man. As he learned the ins and outs of gymnastics from his coach Sam James, his early training sessions were a combination of intense practice and exciting exploration. During those formative years, he relied heavily on his family, especially his parents, Brian and Madeleine. They made it possible for Max to follow his heart by giving him the support and tools he needed.

When Max initially started competing, it was at the regional and local levels. His self-assurance and skill set were greatly enhanced by these contests. His strength, precision, and artistic flair would later become his trademarks, and he became famous for them fast. The gymnastics community came to recognize and respect him for his consistently outstanding performances. Mental toughness and resilience, which are crucial for any athlete striving for greatness, were also lessons Max learned from these early contests.

Participating in the UK National Gymnastics Championships was one of Max's earliest major accomplishments. His success in this tournament demonstrated his immense talent. Max, who was one of the youngest competitors, impressed the judges and spectators with his outstanding skills, resulting in high scores. This win was a watershed moment; it solidified his faith in his abilities and spurred him on to greater strenuous training.

Max accrued more and more accomplishments as he persisted in competing. His strong showings in numerous junior national and international competitions helped him earn a reputation as a serious contender. He won a slew of medals and honors thanks to his natural talent and his commitment to training. His loved ones, coaches, and the gymnastics world at large could all take pride in these accomplishments, which were more than simply personal triumphs for him.

Taking part in the European Junior Championships was a high point for Max during his junior career. On a grand stage, Max displayed his talent and poise while competing against the top young gymnasts from all over Europe. His remarkable performances garnered him numerous medals and cemented his status as one of the world's most promising young gymnasts. As a taste of the international gymnastics circuit and preparation for what was to come, Max's experience competing at such a high level was priceless.

Max endured arduous and punishing training throughout his junior year. Scott Hann, Max's coach at South Essex Gymnastics Club, had his training sessions carefully scheduled so that he could reach his full potential. The development of Max was greatly aided by Scott Hann's coaching style, which combines technical precision with motivational support. A strong relationship based on mutual regard and a common goal of achievement developed between coach and athlete over the years.

Max never wavered in his commitment to gymnastics. Hours of practice, conditioning, and skill refinement were often part of his daily routines, which demonstrated his commitment. Impressively, he managed his time wisely and kept up with both his training and his academic obligations. His parents were always there to back Max, and they made sure he had all the resources he needed to be successful in gymnastics and in the classroom. Max found the self-assurance and drive to keep going because of their steadfast faith in his abilities.

Max started planning his move to the senior level as his junior year continued. Competing against more seasoned and technically gifted athletes is an essential part of any gymnast's transition. The transition to senior-level gymnastics was an exhilarating and intimidating experience for Max. Despite knowing there would be obstacles, he was resolute in his pursuit of even greater success.

Just as he had shown in his junior years, Max dove headfirst into his first experiences at the senior level. Recognizing that the change would necessitate adjustment and persistence, he approached each competition with an eye toward learning and improvement. Although he was up against more formidable opponents, he never stopped impressing with his extraordinary talent and work ethic, and his performances were praiseworthy.

The capacity to keep his feet firmly planted on the ground and his mind on the task at hand was crucial to Max's smooth progression to senior-level gymnastics. His early successes didn't make him forget the value of working hard and always trying to get better. With the help of his coach Scott Hann, he was able to overcome the obstacles presented by senior-level competition. To make sure everything went smoothly, Max and Scott were very understanding and trustworthy with one another.

Max also had a number of introspective turning points as he progressed from junior to senior status. He improved both athletically and personally with every match, practice, and victory. Because of these things, he is very disciplined, very resilient, and very driven to succeed. Max's life is an inspiring testament to the principles and values that were inculcated in him from an early age, as well as his remarkable talent.

In conclusion, Max Whitlock's junior year performance reflects his early talent, perseverance, and strong support system. From his humble beginnings at the Sapphire School of Gymnastics to his stellar performances at the national and international levels, Max's story is one of relentless dedication and incredible accomplishments. Learning, adapting, and constantly improving were hallmarks of the crucial transition to senior-level gymnastics. Success in this endeavor was due in large part to Max's personal resolve, as well as to the encouragement and advice of his family and coaches. Gaining insight into Max Whitlock's formative years puts his later accomplishments in a human perspective, illuminating the significance of family, passion, and commitment to his path.

CHAPTER 3 :SENIOR CAREER: THE RISE TO PROMINENCE

Max Whitlock's senior gymnastics career is an inspiring tale of tenacity, skill, and record-breaking accomplishments. From his early senior competition days to his current status as a world-renowned gymnast, he overcame many obstacles and reached many milestones.

After a solid junior season, Max Whitlock made the jump to the senior level. Both the level of competition and the stakes were increased. Still, Max brought the same level of focus and energy to this new chapter as he had during his junior year. His first few years of high school competition served as both a learning experience and a platform to display his developing abilities. He could challenge himself and his gymnastics routines at each competition.

At the 2010 European Championships in Birmingham, Max made one of his maiden appearances at the senior level of gymnastics. Max performed admirably despite the added pressure of competing in front of his home crowd. On the pommel horse in particular, he showed off his strength, balance, and technical precision, putting on an outstanding performance. Even though he came up empty at the European Championships, his performance there proved he was a gymnastics superstar on the rise.

The year 2012 was crucial to Max's career because it was when he finally broke through. Max was a dual Olympic competitor, taking part in both the relay and the individual events in London. The home crowd's enthusiasm was tangible, and the energy in London was electric. Max gave an absolutely outstanding performance. He was an integral part of the British gymnastics team that won bronze in the team event, the first Olympic team medal for Great Britain since 1912. Max and British gymnastics as a whole can look back on this accomplishment with pride.

Max kept shining on his own. He became the first male gymnast from the United Kingdom to win an Olympic medal on the pommel horse when he performed to a bronze. This event marked a watershed in his career, catapulting him to stardom and solidifying his position as a dominant figure in the sport. Max was deeply affected by the Olympics, which gave him the self-assurance and motivation to strive for even bigger things.

The London Olympics were a stepping stone to even greater success for Max. World Championships in Antwerp in 2013 were also a watershed moment. The pommel horse event was the most impressive of Max's many competitions. He won a silver medal for his faultless routine. This feat proved he could compete at the highest level and cemented his reputation as a pommel horse expert.

Max overcame many obstacles on his path, despite his successes. Both mental and physical stamina are required to compete at the highest level of gymnastics. Max was not immune to the constant threat of injury. After suffering a shoulder injury in 2014 that necessitated surgery, he encountered a major obstacle. Months of rehabilitation and meticulous management of his training regimen were required on the long road to recovery. Nevertheless, Max was able to overcome this challenging time thanks to his tenacity and resolve. Because of his resilience and dedication to the sport, he was able to recover from an injury and perform at a high level again.

Several outstanding performances marked Max's return to the spotlight. His ability to excel on multiple apparatuses was on full display at the 2014 Glasgow Commonwealth Games, where he took home three golds and two silvers. The fact that Max was able to recover from setbacks and perform admirably under pressure made this victory all the more significant.

Max reached yet another major milestone the following year, in 2015, at the Glasgow World Championships. As the first gymnast from the United Kingdom to ever win a world championship in the pommel horse event, he took home the gold medal. This triumph validated Max's position as one of the world's top pommel horse specialists and was the result of his years of hard work and devotion. His routine was so well-executed that it proved without a shadow of a doubt that he was the best in the world.

Max's ascent to fame persisted unchecked. There was a turning point in his career during the 2016 Olympics in Rio. Max displayed exceptional skill in a variety of gymnastic events while competing against the world's top gymnasts. He was a two-time gold medalist, having excelled in both the floor exercise and the pommel horse. The first British gymnast to ever win back-to-back gold medals at the Olympics, Max's triumphs were historic. He had worked tirelessly for years, and his performance in Rio was the reward for all that effort.

Max encountered many obstacles during his senior year, but he overcame them all by focusing his determination and honing his abilities. A critical component of his success has been his capacity to triumph over adversity, be it physical harm, intense rivalry, or the demands of performing on a global scale. The significance of having a solid support system and the power of persistence are both demonstrated by Max's journey. He owes a great debt of gratitude to his loved ones, coaches, and teammates for being there for him through the highs and lows of his professional gymnastics career.

It is a testament to Max Whitlock's talent, perseverance, and hard work that he rose to prominence in his senior career. Everything that Max has accomplished, from his early senior competitions to his breakthrough performances and the important milestones along the way, is a testament to the power of perseverance and a thirst for greatness. As a result of his successes, he has become a personal icon and an inspiration to gymnasts all over the world, including in the United Kingdom. Max's stellar reputation in the sport is the product of his dogged pursuit of excellence and his refusal to settle for anything less than the best.

CHAPTER 4: OLYMPIC JOURNEY

The incredible Olympic journey of Max Whitlock is an inspiring tale of perseverance, commitment, and greatness. This biography follows him as he competes in three crucial Olympic Games: London 2012, Rio 2016, and Tokyo 2020. It details his training, tactics, and preparation for each event.

An historic event for British gymnastics, the 2012 London Olympics marked the beginning of Max's Olympic journey. Max, a young gymnast at the time, approached the Games with a combination of humility and determination, despite the obvious excitement and pressure of competing in his home country. He was very methodical and thorough in his preparation for London. He had to win a slew of national and international competitions, showing that he could hold his own against the top gymnasts in the world if he wanted to make it to the Olympics. He achieved a personal triumph by qualifying, but British gymnastics took a giant leap forward, heralding the emergence of fresh talent.

There was an electric vibe in London. The overwhelming support from the home crowd served as an extra source of motivation as well as pressure. Max's performances showcased his dedication and perseverance. Among his many events, his performances in the team and individual all-around contests were particularly noteworthy. In their pursuit of history, the British men's gymnastics team encountered intense rivalry. The squad won bronze, Britain's first medal in a hundred years, thanks in large part to Max's efforts. Everyone in British gymnastics, not only Max, saw this as a huge step forward, and they celebrated it accordingly.

When it came to the pommel horse, Max stood out as an individual. The technical demands of the pommel horse, a gymnast's strength, balance, and accuracy are well-known. Max won bronze medal for his flawless performance of the routine. He became the first male gymnast from the United Kingdom to win an Olympic medal with this singular achievement, which showcased his talent and paved the way for his subsequent triumphs.

The 2016 Summer Olympics in Rio were a watershed point for Max. Expectations were through the roof since he had already become a major player in the gymnastics world. He trained intensely and according to a strict schedule in anticipation of Rio. The difficulty of Max's routines and his execution were his primary concerns. To prepare for the intense scrutiny of the Olympic stage, he collaborated closely with his coaches to hone every aspect of his performance.

Max gave an absolutely outstanding performance in Rio. His floor and pommel horse routines stood out among the many that he entered. He demonstrated his versatility as a gymnast with a floor exercise that combined power, grace, and precision. Max became the first British gymnast to ever win an Olympic gold medal with a perfectly executed routine. Years of preparation and perseverance had paid off at this point.

In Rio, Max's performance on the pommel horse cemented his position as a gymnast of the highest caliber. Despite how difficult the routine was, Max executed it with such assurance and grace. He won yet another gold medal for his almost flawless execution. His hard work and preparation had paid off, and this accomplishment was proof of that. As a result of his unprecedented double gold in Rio, Max is now considered one of Britain's all-time great gymnasts.

In Rio, Max's Olympic adventure was far from over. There were new opportunities and problems brought about by the pandemic that forced the 2020 Summer Olympics to be postponed to 2021 in Tokyo. Because the pandemic interrupted regular training schedules and added uncertainty, the Tokyo preparations were unlike any other. But Max and his squad became creative, training in new and different ways while maintaining their concentration. Keeping physically fit, honing his routines, and mentally resilient in the face of unprecedented circumstances were all part of his preparation.

While in Tokyo, Max planned to carry on his father's work. His performances exhibited the same level of commitment and brilliance that had characterized his entire career. Once again, Max encountered fierce competition while riding the pommel horse. Everyone was waiting for his routine, and he delivered it with the usual flair and accuracy. His performance showcased his unwavering talent and determination, even though he did not win a medal.

The Olympic journey of Max Whitlock is a complex web of aspiration, perseverance, and remarkable success. The qualities of a world-class athlete have been on full display throughout Max's career, beginning with his debut in London, when he helped end a hundred-year drought for British gymnastics, continuing with his historic double gold in Rio and his resolute performance in Tokyo. His story is about more than gymnastics medals and recognition; it's about his dogged quest of perfection and the motivation he gives to other athletes.

Dedication, perseverance, and the steadfast backing of a solid team are powerfully demonstrated in Max's story. Thanks to him, British gymnastics is now more well-known around the world, and he has motivated many young athletes. Max will go down in history as one of the top gymnasts of all time, and his impact will be felt for decades to come. He is just getting started on his journey.

CHAPTER 5: WORLD CHAMPIONSHIP AND OTHER MAJOR COMPETITIONS

Max Whitlock's success at the World Championships and other major competitions is evidence of his talent, perseverance, and ability to overcome adversity. Every milestone he has achieved on the global stage has added to the impressive fabric of his legendary career. This narrative delves into his involvement in various prestigious international competitions, providing a detailed and relatable account of his experiences and accomplishments.

A string of outstanding performances during Max Whitlock's entry into the World Championships has established him as one of gymnastics' top performers. In 2013, he made his big debut at the Antwerp World Championships. Max demonstrated his potential by winning bronze on the pommel horse, even though he is still a rookie on the senior international circuit. This feat marked a watershed moment, heralding his entry onto the global arena and suggesting his future greatness.

Max continued to improve his consistency and overall performance at the World Championships in the years that followed. He won silver in the pommel horse event at the 2014 World Championships in Nanning, China, proving his mettle once again. Competing against the best gymnasts in the world, this event was an extreme test of strength and stamina. The fact that Max kept his cool and performed his routine perfectly even when the stakes were high showed how hard he had trained and how strong his mind was.

Max had a memorable World Championship experience in Glasgow in 2015. He turned in a career-defining performance while competing at home. The encouragement of his hometown crowd and his own drive to succeed helped him take first place on the pommel horse. It was a watershed moment for British gymnastics, as it was the first time a male gymnast from the country had ever won a gold medal at the World Championships; the win was also a personal triumph.

At the 2017 World Championships in Montreal, Max maintained his winning streak and solidified his dominance on the pommel horse. There was never any question about his status as the sport's elite after witnessing his performance, which was a showcase of precision and artistry. His dogged determination and obsession with perfection were on full display when he won gold medals at the World Championships in consecutive years.

Max Whitlock's story is one of extraordinary accomplishments and continuous success not only at the World Championships but also at the European Championships. In 2012, he achieved his maiden major accomplishment at the European level when he and his team won silver. He would go on to dominate the competition, and this early success was just the beginning.

With his pommel horse gold medal in 2013, Max finally won an individual European title. He proved he could compete and win at the highest level in Europe with this victory, so it was significant. Max has maintained his impressive form at the European Championships, where he has won medals in a variety of apparatus events. He is one of the most decorated gymnasts in the history of the European Championships thanks to his versatility and consistency.

A large portion of Max Whitlock's professional life has revolved around the Commonwealth Games. In 2010, in Delhi, Max made his Commonwealth Games debut, representing England. The English team won silver in the team event thanks in large part to his outstanding performances, even though he was still a young athlete.

A turning point in Max's life came during the 2014 Glasgow Commonwealth Games. He won first place in three separate events—the all-around, the floor exercise, and the pommel horse—after a string of outstanding performances. His performance at Glasgow demonstrated his maturation as a gymnast. His versatility and ability to excel across different apparatus were demonstrated by the multiple gold medals he won.

The fact that Max took part in the 2018 Gold Coast Commonwealth Games only served to cement his place in history. Again, he came through in a big way, this time taking first place in the team event and gold on the pommel horse. His accomplishments at the Commonwealth Games have brought great honor to England and served as an inspiration to aspiring gymnasts of the next generation.

Along with these important competitions, Max Whitlock has participated in a plethora of other international events, all of which have helped him grow and succeed as a gymnast. For example, Max has been able to refine his abilities and acquire significant experience through the World Cup series. His results in these tournaments have frequently served as a taste of what's to come in his major championship campaigns.

Max has had a string of outstanding performances throughout his time at the World Cup. He has shown that he can compete at a high level across various apparatus by finishing on the podium consistently. To keep himself at the top of his game, he has taken advantage of the opportunity to compete in these events to try out new routines and hone his techniques.

There have been many obstacles on Max's path through these contests. For example, injuries have been a major obstacle. But Max has always been able to come back stronger, thanks to his resilience and determination. His mental fortitude and unwavering commitment to the sport allow him to persevere through challenges and maintain his exceptional performance.

There are a number of reasons why Max has been so successful on the global stage. For example, one important factor has been his intense training program. Training with dedication and focus has always been a priority for Max. Everything about his regimen is calculated to play to his strengths and hide his weaknesses.

The encouragement of his teammates and coaches has also been important. Coaches have been instrumental in Max's success, and he has frequently acknowledged this. Their advice, insight, and support have been priceless. His family's encouragement has also been crucial. Max has frequently mentioned that his family has been there for him every step of the way, offering encouragement and support.

The incredible journey of Max Whitlock through numerous international competitions, including the Commonwealth Games, the World Championships, and the European Championships, is a testament to his unwavering commitment, resilience, and remarkable accomplishments. Not only has he achieved personal success as a result of his performances, but British gymnastics has also become more well-known internationally. Max left an indelible mark on the world by proving that anything is possible with dedication, perseverance, and an obsession with perfection.

Inspiring future gymnasts, Max's accomplishments shine a light on his path. His life serves as an inspiring example of the value of sticking with something until you achieve your goals. The influence of Max Whitlock on the sport will last for years to come, and his legacy is well-established.

CHAPTER 6: SIGNATURE SKILLS AND TECHNIQUES

Throughout his gymnastics career, Max Whitlock has been known for his unique style and groundbreaking innovations, especially on the pommel horse. He is one of the best gymnasts of all time thanks to his unique style and the amount of time he spends training. This biography explores Whitlock's distinctive abilities by looking at his distinctive gymnastic style, innovations in pommel horse techniques, and the daily routines and training programs that molded his impressive career.

The gymnastic style of Max Whitlock is defined by a combination of strength, grace, and accuracy. He painstakingly designs his pommel horse routines, floor exercises, and other apparatuses to highlight his strengths and downplay his weaknesses. The remarkable control and balance that Whitlock possesses is one of the most eye-catching features of his style. He maintains a high level of difficulty without sacrificing execution, as evidenced by the seamless transitions between complex elements in his routines.

Whitlock has a unique style that stands out on the pommel horse. His routines are visually stunning and technically demanding because he has a special knack for blending traditional methods with modern touches. Known as "circles," his routines frequently showcase a succession of swift and extremely precise circular motions. He builds momentum and sets up more complex skills on these circles, which are the foundation of many of his routines.

The addition of new and more challenging skills is one of the most significant innovations that Whitlock has introduced to the pommel horse. One impressive move he's perfected is the "Thomas flair," in which he performs a succession of wide swings with his legs outstretched, showcasing his incredible agility and poise. This spin, along with other complex moves like the "handstand pirouette," has become Whitlock's trademark and a major differentiator in the world of gymnastics.

Not only is Whitlock skilled, but his ability to innovate on the pommel horse is a reflection of his extensive knowledge of the apparatus. He effortlessly executes these challenging elements by playing to his strengths, which include strong upper body stability and core stability. He strikes a delicate balance between difficulty and execution in his routines so that he can achieve the highest possible scores.

The basis of Whitlock's achievements is his consistent and intense training programs. Consistency and small, steady gains are the cornerstones of his rigorous training regimen. Several sessions per day, lasting several hours each, make up Whitlock's training routine. Strength training, flexibility exercises, and technical drills are all part of these sessions' plans to improve his performance.

Part of Whitlock's routine that is absolutely essential is strength training. To prepare for the explosive and fluid movements demanded by gymnastics, he uses a wide range of exercises to strengthen his upper and lower bodies. He trains for power and endurance through weightlifting, bodyweight exercises, and resistance training.

Another important part of Whitlock's training is to be flexible. A great deal of mobility, especially in the back, shoulders, and hips, is necessary for gymnastics. To make sure he can execute all the various motions required by his routines, Whitlock spends a lot of time in training on mobility and stretching. He is able to keep performing at a high level throughout his career thanks to his flexibility, which also helps him avoid injuries.

Whitlock focuses his training sessions on technical drills. The purpose of these drills is to hone his abilities and guarantee that he performs his routines precisely. This is done on a pommel horse by practicing certain steps until they are perfected. Whitlock takes great care in these drills, dissecting each movement into its constituent pieces and honing them one by one. His meticulousness is on full display.

Whitlock stresses mental preparation as much as physical training. Gymnastics is a sport that places tremendous mental demands on its participants, necessitating concentration, self-control, and perseverance. Whitlock uses methods like regular mental rehearsals, mindfulness practices, and visualization exercises to keep his mind sharp and manage stress. Using these methods, he is able to maintain composure and give his all during competitions.

Whitlock makes sure to incorporate both training and recovery into his daily routines. After putting his body through the rigorous physical demands of training, he knows how important it is to give it a break. A good night's sleep, a balanced diet, and recovery techniques like massage and physiotherapy are all part of this. Whitlock stays consistent in his training and stays away from burnout by making recovery a top priority.

Max Whitlock's incredible journey in gymnastics showcases his unwavering commitment, creative thinking, and thirst for perfection. He revolutionized gymnastics with his innovative technique, especially on the pommel horse. He has made technically excellent and visually stunning routines by integrating traditional methods with revolutionary innovations. The bedrock of his success is his rigorous training regimens and disciplined daily routines, which enable him to consistently perform at the highest level.

The influence of Whitlock on gymnastics goes far beyond his own accomplishments. By showing what is achievable through dedication, creativity, and persistence, he has motivated a new wave of gymnasts to reach their full potential. Aspiring athletes look up to his method of playing the sport, which is marked by thorough training and a dedication to always getting better.

Max Whitlock will surely leave an indelible mark on gymnastics as he continues his career. He made an everlasting impression on the sport through his innovative technical contributions and impressive competitive achievements. In their pursuit of gymnastics greatness, aspiring gymnasts will look up to Whitlock as an inspiration. His life serves as a potent lesson in the value of perseverance, commitment, and the never-ending quest for greatness.

CHAPTER 7: COACHING AND MENTORSHIP

Max Whitlock did not embark on his path to gymnastics icondom on his own. Relationships with coaches and mentors, who have offered him advice, encouragement, and knowledge throughout his career, have been pivotal in determining his trajectory. Whitlock has also started to give back to gymnastics by helping young gymnasts grow into their potential and guaranteeing the sport's continued success in Britain.

One of the keys to Whitlock's success has been the rapport he has built with his coaches. His potential was genuinely fostered by the guidance of seasoned coaches, although he displayed promise from an early age. Gymnasts and their coaches form an unbreakable bond based on mutual respect, commitment, and trust. An important part of Whitlock's career has been his ongoing partnership with Scott Hann. Reputable British gymnastics figure Hann saw Whitlock's potential early on and devoted himself to helping him grow and improve.

The strength of the bond between coach and athlete is demonstrated by their partnership. Mental toughness, resilience, and strategic thinking are just as important as physical preparation, according to Hann's coaching philosophy. He made sure that Whitlock was constantly improving as an athlete by customizing his training programs to play to his strengths and fix his weaknesses. Because of this dynamic, Whitlock was able to continuously raise the bar for his performance, which led to his historic accomplishments on the global stage.

Beyond Whitlock's immediate coaching staff, mentors have had a significant impact on his career. He has looked to many people and places for direction and inspiration throughout his journey. He has been able to stay focused and motivated despite the difficulties of elite competition thanks to the varied viewpoints offered by his mentors. He credits his father, who taught him the importance of working hard and never giving up, as a significant influence in his life. A continual source of motivation for him has been his father's unfaltering support and encouragement.

Also, Whitlock has found motivation from the lives of former gymnasts who went on to accomplish remarkable things. He learned what it takes to succeed at the highest level by studying the careers of greats like Nadia Comăneci and Kohei Uchimura. Even though they weren't always involved in his training, these coaches have shaped his perspective on the sport and his goals for the future.

Whitlock started to see himself more and more as a mentor as his career developed. Realizing how much his coaches meant to him, he wanted to pay it forward by helping train gymnasts of the future. His life's ups and downs have given him the tools he needs to help aspiring gymnasts succeed.

Through his involvement in gymnastics programs and initiatives that support emerging athletes, Whitlock demonstrates his dedication to nurturing young talent. Participating in training camps, seminars, and clinics on a regular basis allows him to share his expertise with aspiring gymnasts. He gives these athletes invaluable insight into competing at the highest levels of their sport through his presence and advice.

The value of tenacity and determination is something that Whitlock stresses to her young gymnasts. To show that there is no certain way to achieve success, he candidly discusses the obstacles he has encountered, such as injuries and failures. He hopes to arm the next generation of athletes with the mental fortitude and resilience to face the challenges of elite competition.

Furthermore, Whitlock's method of mentoring extends beyond merely imparting technical know-how. He thinks athletes should focus on both their athletic and academic pursuits, and he urges them to strike a balance between the two. This all-encompassing method guarantees that young gymnasts are ready for more than just their athletic careers; they are also given the tools and mindset to thrive in life off the mat.

As a mentor, Whitlock stresses the value of a welcoming and accepting classroom setting. In his view, the most important thing for the growth of athletes is to create a welcoming environment where they feel appreciated and encouraged. This outlook is congruent with his life experiences, in which the support and faith of his teachers and coaches were critical to his achievement.

Through his involvement with national and international organizations, Whitlock's influence reaches far beyond the gymnastics community. He promotes gymnastics and fights for athletes' rights by working closely with governing bodies. Being an ambassador and role model for gymnastics gives him the power to motivate the next generation and make a difference.

Expanding gymnastics opportunities for youth from underrepresented groups is a cause near and dear to

Whitlock's heart. Recognizing that aspirational gymnasts may face social and financial obstacles, he is determined to remove these obstacles. He ensures that gymnastics can be a lifelong passion for all kids by supporting programs that give resources, training, and scholarships to disadvantaged youth through partnerships with organizations and foundations.

A shining example of the transformative power of coaching, mentoring, and altruism is Whitlock's meteoric rise from promising young gymnast to legendary champion and mentor. He owes his success to the relationships he's built with coaches and mentors, who have provided him with the knowledge, encouragement, and direction he needed to excel at the highest level of his sport. Because of his dedication to mentoring up-and-coming gymnasts and spreading the principles of grit, determination, and self-improvement, his legacy will live on and encourage other athletes to follow in his footsteps.

CHAPTER 8:PERSONAL LIFE

The story of Max Whitlock's life outside of gymnastics is just as interesting and motivating. The many threads that make up Whitlock's life—his family and personal relationships, his interests and hobbies outside of gymnastics, his public image, and his media presence—add to his renowned humility and grounded nature.

Max Whitlock's life is built upon his family and personal relationships. Whitlock has consistently expressed gratitude to his family, who were his rock during his gymnastics career, and was born in Hemel Hempstead, Hertfordshire. The support of his parents, Brian and Madeleine Whitlock, has been invaluable to him. Everyone has been involved, from picking him up from early morning practices to cheering him on at competitions. Max was able to confidently and diligently pursue his dreams because of the solid foundation they provided through their support.

Leah Hickton, Whitlock's wife, and their relationship is another important part of his private life. They tied the knot in 2017 after meeting as young gymnasts. As someone who has been on the gymnastics team before, Leah has a great grasp of the sport and is always there to cheer you on. Willow, their daughter, was born to them in 2019, and she brought an abundance of joy into their lives. As a father and athlete, Whitlock's sense of duty and drive has been strengthened by the birth of his daughter Willow.

Whitlock values harmony in his family life and places a premium on quality time spent together. He still manages to fit in quality time with his family and friends despite his busy training and competition schedule. The importance he places on family is a reflection of the principles of unity, love, and support that have guided his life. The emotional sustenance he needs to succeed in his professional pursuits comes from moments like spending time with his family or having a peaceful night at home.

Max Whitlock has a wide range of interests and hobbies outside of gymnastics that he uses to relax and keep himself grounded. Football is a sport that he loves. Whitlock has been a lifelong fan of West Ham United and takes pleasure in both watching and playing the sport on occasion for fun. He finds that football is a great way to relax and enjoy a new type of athletic challenge, which is much needed after the intense world of gymnastics.

Whitlock is just as passionate about music as he is about football. He finds comfort and inspiration in the rhythms and melodies of music from all over the world, which he enjoys listening to. Additionally, his training routines would not be complete without music, which serves to energize and concentrate him while he works out. Even though his athletic career is demanding, it provides him with a personal escape where he can express himself and find calm.

Fitness goes beyond gymnastics for Whitlock. In order to keep himself fit and healthy, he does a variety of exercises, such as running and strength training. He believes that a healthy lifestyle is crucial for longevity in sport and life, and this holistic approach to fitness highlights his commitment to that belief.

Beyond the gym, he also has a passion for nutrition and good food. Whitlock knows that in order to perform at his best, he needs to fuel his body with a well-rounded diet. He frequently updates his social media followers on his culinary adventures, which include trying out new cuisines and healthy recipes. His goal in prioritizing health and wellness is twofold: first, to improve his athletic performance; and second, to encourage others to do the same.

Max Whitlock's media persona and public persona are reflections of his individual and athletic personas. Whitlock has widespread esteem among his contemporaries, fans, and media due to his modesty, honesty, and sportsmanship. His humble and friendly nature has won him many fans and made him a legend in British sports.

Whitlock's eagerness to interact with fans and divulge life and career secrets is a defining feature of his media presence. He shares bits and pieces of his training regimen, family life, and interests on social media. His followers value his honesty and relatability, which he has achieved through his openness and transparency.

There has been a lot of coverage of Whitlock's character and values in addition to his accomplishments in the media. It is common to hear accounts of his humility, commitment, and perseverance, which give the impression of an athlete who is rooted in his principles, talented, and dedicated to his work. The public has a more favorable impression of Whitlock because of his dedication to giving back to the community and his poise when faced with success.

Whitlock is very involved in a number of community projects and charitable endeavors in addition to his work with the press. He uses his celebrity to advocate for causes that benefit young people, particularly in the areas of health, education, and athletics. He wants to repay the community that has helped him succeed professionally, so he gets involved in charitable work. Whitlock has made a significant impact outside of gymnastics, whether it's through school visits to motivate young athletes or participating in fundraising events.

Whitlock, as an example for young athletes and fans, is very conscious of the impact he has. He hopes to inspire others to follow their passions and be honest in the process by being an example of what it means to live a life of purpose. The principles that have guided him throughout his journey—the importance of working hard, being resilient, and keeping a balanced perspective—are frequently emphasized in his messages.

Finally, Max Whitlock's private life is a complex web of affection, service, and striving for greatness. He has been able to accomplish extraordinary things in gymnastics because of the support he has received from his family and friends. His balance and joy are enhanced by his hobbies and interests outside of sports, which contribute to his overall well-being. The principles of modesty, honesty, and selflessness that characterize him as a person and a sportsman are also reflected in his public persona and interactions with the media. Whitlock has left an impression on the world that goes far beyond his gymnastics accomplishments because of the way he lives his life.

CHAPTER 9: CHALLENGES AND OVERCOMING ADVERSITY

The story of Max Whitlock's rise to gymnastics greatness is one of overcoming adversity and emerging victorious, but it is also full of victories and medals. Pain, mental struggles, and unwavering networks of support have all been threads in his career tapestry.

Like any top athlete, Max Whitlock has had to deal with injuries throughout his career. He has tested his determination and persevered through numerous physical obstacles on his gymnastics journey. A ripped calf muscle in 2014 was one of the most serious injuries he ever suffered. This setback occurred at a crucial juncture, right before important competitions, and it almost derailed his career. There was a lot of physical pain, but there was also a tremendous mental toll. His mind was consumed by the weight of recovery's unknowns and the dread of falling short of his previous level of performance.

The road to recovery after suffering such an injury is long and winding. Whitlock has always been very methodical and focused when it comes to rehabilitation. He wholeheartedly committed to his physical therapy, strength training, and conditioning regimen. His days were planned around rigorous rehabilitation sessions, where he would work on both healing his injury and building strength to avoid such problems in the future. A long and winding road of gradual improvement interspersed with occasional setbacks marked the path to recovery. However, he overcame this difficult period by staying focused on his goal of playing the sport he loves again. His determination was evident.

Max Whitlock, like any other high-performing athlete, deals with psychological issues on the side. An intricate psychological terrain is created by the demands of continuous peak performance, the anticipation of spectators and the press, and the intrinsic motivation to achieve greatness. Whitlock struggled with performance anxiety, which was a big psychological barrier. Athletes' mental health and performance can take a hit when they're under extreme pressure to perform well and terrified of failing.

In order to triumph over these mental obstacles, Whitlock has employed a multipronged approach. He now incorporates mindfulness and meditation into his daily life. These practices assist him in remaining centered, controlling his stress levels, and preserving his mental clarity. Anxieties and self-confidence are both helped by visualizing his routines and performances going well, so visualization techniques play an important role as well. These mental drills help him stay composed and focused during competitions, which is just as important as his physical training.

Whitlock has been able to weather the storms of his career with the aid of coping strategies and social networks. The people closest to him, like his wife Leah, have always been there for him. The emotional groundwork is solid because Leah knows what gymnastics is like and she always cheers you on. Because of the foundation of trust and understanding they've laid in their relationship, Whitlock feels comfortable enough to talk to them about his struggles.

His coaching staff is just as important as his family. Scott Hann, who has coached him for many years, has been an invaluable resource for him, both in terms of strategy and in terms of adapting to new situations. Hann's faith in Whitlock and his skill at motivating him to his full potential were crucial to his achievement. The foundation of the coach-athlete relationship is a shared goal of success as well as an atmosphere of trust and respect.

When faced with adversity, Whitlock reaches out to more people than just his inner circle for help. To prepare himself mentally for the stresses of competition, he has collaborated with sports psychologists. These experts provide methods for dealing with stress, boosting self-esteem, and keeping one's concentration. By following their advice, he is able to keep his emotions in check and his physical health in top shape.

Whitlock also receives one-of-a-kind encouragement from his interactions with gymnastics fans and the wider community. The support and adulation from his followers keeps him going and serves as a constant reminder of the significance of his accomplishments. He frequently engages his followers in conversation by sharing personal experiences and struggles on social media. His journey is made more relatable and meaningful through this candor, which also gives him a sense of belonging and common goal.

The fact that Whitlock has shown he can adapt and evolve despite hardship is more evidence of his resilience. Because of his history of injuries and setbacks, he is always evaluating and adjusting his training programs. Recognizing the significance of rest and recuperation, he has learnt to pay attention to his body. Because of the harsh and unforgiving physical demands of the sport, this flexibility is essential.

Whitlock stays at the top of his game by adopting a holistic approach to training and recovery.

His devotion to the sport is also an important part of his coping mechanism. His enthusiasm for gymnastics has remained unwavering through all of the difficulties. He is able to persevere in the face of hardship because of this inner drive. As evidence of his passion, he has devoted himself entirely to honing his skills and has never stopped striving for greatness. His unwavering determination to succeed is fueled by his profound passion for gymnastics, which propels him to conquer challenges and pursue excellence.

The story of Whitlock also shows how important it is to have a support system. His contributions as a coach and a gymnast have made him an indispensable member of the British gymnastics community. His involvement in grassroots initiatives and interactions with younger gymnasts demonstrate his dedication to giving back. Both he and the next generation benefit from his willingness to share what he has learned, which has helped him stay strong. A great strength is the sense of belonging and purpose that this community provides.

Last but not least, the story of Max Whitlock's journey through hardship is an inspiring one of perseverance, resolve, and constant encouragement. The fact that he was able to overcome his injuries and recover so well speaks volumes about his strength of character. The mental obstacles he encounters illustrate how difficult it is to consistently perform at a high level in professional athletics. A multi-faceted approach is necessary to navigate the highs and lows of an athletic career, and his coping mechanisms, which are based on mindfulness, support systems, and a deep passion for gymnastics, demonstrate this. Whitlock, despite everything, is an inspiration because she never stops challenging the limits of gymnastics.

CHAPTER 10: AWARDS AND HONORS

Max Whitlock has made tremendous contributions to gymnastics in Britain and around the world, and his impressive resume is a testament to that. He is one of the most decorated gymnasts of his generation, having won numerous national and international accolades for his accomplishments.

It all started early in Whitlock's career when he set out to earn these accolades. He became famous for his exceptional gymnastics performances due to his commitment, accuracy, and reliability. He was so dominant in British gymnastics that he received national recognitions. Whitlock has won the British Championships on many occasions, most notably in the all-around, pommel horse, and floor exercise divisions. His versatility and ability to maintain peak performance across different apparatus are evident in these victories.

His worldwide achievements solidify his place in history. Whitlock has been absolutely sensational in the World Championships. His signature event, the pommel horse, is where he has earned the most medals, including multiple golds. Gymnastics federations around the world have recognized his innovative routines and technical skill, which have raised the bar for the sport.

Among Whitlock's most notable achievements was his sweep of the floor exercise, pommel horse, and all-around bronze medals at the 2016 Rio Olympics. His feats were celebrated as a watershed moment for British gymnastics, and he became the first gymnast from his country to ever win gold in these events. His Olympic victory was a watershed moment in the public's view and enthusiasm for gymnastics in the United Kingdom, and it was a cause for national celebration as well.

Whitlock has received a plethora of honors and decorations from different organizations, on top of his Olympic accomplishments. In 2017, he was honoured for his contributions to gymnastics by being appointed Member of the Order of the British Empire (MBE). Not only has he excelled as a gymnast, but he has also been an incredible role model for young gymnasts all over the world, and this award is a testament to that.

Despite his low medal total, Whitlock had a significant influence on British gymnastics. The innovative drive and capacity to raise the sport's profile are hallmarks of his legacy. British gymnastics had not enjoyed such uninterrupted global success prior to his rise to prominence. By setting an example of perseverance and brilliance, Whitlock has opened doors for other gymnasts to follow.

The growing popularity and financial support of gymnastics in the United Kingdom are further evidence of his impact. Many young people have been motivated to pursue athletics by his achievements, and he has played an active role in grassroots programs that have helped develop promising athletes. Aspiring gymnasts can learn from Whitlock's passion and experience at his frequent coaching clinics and workshops. His dedication to community service guarantees that his impact will be felt long after he stops competing in gymnastics.

Another important factor in Whitlock's legacy is his public persona and the amount of time he spent in the media. He has won the hearts of both fans and fellow athletes with his modesty, work ethic, and friendly personality. His candor regarding the difficulties and demands of being a top athlete has shed light on the truth of competing at a high level. Whitlock has made the sport more approachable by bringing a human element to it through his stories.

He has become a national icon in part because his accomplishments have been chronicled in the media. Gymnastics has benefited from Whitlock's appearances on television and social media, among other platforms. His story, the value of mental health, and the perseverance needed to reach the top have all been featured in interviews and documentaries. In addition to recognizing his achievements, these engagements have shed light on the complexities and demands of the sport.

The honors bestowed upon Whitlock by various sports organizations are further proof of his impact. The esteemed BBC Sports Personality of the Year award was among many that he has received nominations for and ultimately won. These honors demonstrate how much of an influence he has had on the sports world as a whole and how he can motivate people from all walks of life.

Whitlock has left an extensive and varied mark on British gymnastics. It covers all he accomplished, from promoting gymnastics to helping train the next generation of athletes. His rise to fame as a gymnast from humble beginnings in Hemel Hempstead is an inspiring tale of grit, determination, and success. Both British gymnastics and the sport of gymnastics as a whole owe a great debt to him for the improvements he brought about.

Looking back on Max Whitlock's career, it's easy to see that the accolades he received were far from insignificant. They stand for the impact of a single athlete's commitment to his sport and his quest for greatness. Aspiring gymnasts look up to Whitlock as an example of the great things that can happen when one follows one's dreams and works tirelessly. Inspiring and motivating generations to come, his story will ensure that his contributions to gymnastics are remembered.

CHAPTER 11:PHILANTHROPY AND COMMUNITY INVOLVEMENT

Max Whitlock's influence goes well beyond the gymnasium, but his rise from a young gymnast to a worldwide superstar is motivational in and of itself. Along with his athletic accomplishments, his charitable work and dedication to community involvement showcase his depth of character. Many people's lives have been touched by Whitlock's commitment to giving back, supporting charitable causes, and championing gymnastics and sports in general.

The fact that Whitlock gives back to the community shows how selfless he is and how much he wants to use his celebrity for good. Many charitable endeavors have brought him joy over the years, and he has always done his best to back causes that mean a lot to him. For instance, through his involvement with the Make-A-Wish Foundation, he has contributed to the realization of the wishes of children dealing with life-threatening illnesses. In addition to giving the kids an experience they will never forget, his interactions with them give them hope and encouragement when they are going through tough times. Whitlock's dedication to making a difference is on full display in these instances, as is his real concern and empathy.

Whitlock has donated to a plethora of different nonprofits, including Make-A-Wish. To help support different causes, he has taken part in auctions, charity runs, and other fundraising events, frequently donating personal items. His participation in these shows that he knows how important it is to use his fame and fortune to help people less fortunate. Many people's lives have been touched by Whitlock's efforts, whether they are to promote understanding of mental health, fund cancer research, or support children's charities.

One of Whitlock's off-the-field pillars is his involvement in the community. He understands the value of maintaining relationships with the people who have helped him succeed professionally. Whitlock frequently makes appearances at community centers, gymnastics clubs, and schools to mentor aspiring athletes and share his story. Because he is friendly and open to talking to fans of all ages, these encounters mean a lot. Young gymnasts looking to follow in Whitlock's footsteps can gain wisdom and inspiration from his story of perseverance through adversity.

The Max Whitlock Gymnastics Club is one of Whitlock's most notable community engagement initiatives. This club was founded with the goal of providing training programs for gymnasts of all abilities in order to make the sport more accessible to kids and teenagers. More than just a name donor, Whitlock is deeply involved with the club, helping to shape training programs and dropping by often to chat with the young gymnasts. This method allows Whitlock to directly mentor and encourage young athletes while also guaranteeing high-quality training. He founded the club because he believed in the life-changing potential of athletics and because he wanted to help the youth of today and tomorrow.

Whitlock also left an important mark through his support of gymnastics and athletics. In addition to its value as a competitive sport, he has long advocated for gymnastics as a way to encourage healthy lifestyle choices and physical fitness. As a result of his lobbying, gymnastics has received more attention and funding in the United Kingdom, which has expanded the sport's reach and appeal. A new generation of gymnasts has been inspired to follow in Whitlock's footsteps by seeing that British gymnasts can compete and succeed on the world stage.

All kinds of sports and physical exercise are something Whitlock is passionate about, not just gymnastics. In his speeches, he has emphasized the value of sports as a means to a healthy lifestyle. He is also an outspoken supporter of efforts to improve mental health, particularly the link between regular exercise and better mental health. For those who are going through the same things, Whitlock's candor about his struggles with mental health and the ways he has dealt with them can be an inspiration.

Whitlock's advocacy work is further impacted by his public persona and the amount of media attention he receives. He spreads good messages about health and sports and uses his platform to call attention to critical issues. He keeps his supporters up-to-date on his whereabouts, charitable work, and advocacy efforts through his robust social media presence. Whitlock reaches out to people outside of the gymnastics community by engaging with a wide audience, amplifying his impact.

Whitlock has shown his character and principles through his advocacy work, community service, and generosity. Both his on-and-off-the-mat accomplishments and his dedication to making a positive impact on the world are exhibited by him. His legacy of kindness, inspiration, and constructive change goes well beyond the honors he has received.

When considering Max Whitlock's life and work, it becomes evident that his influence extends far beyond his gymnastics achievements. He has changed the lives of countless people and made a lasting impact through his philanthropy and community involvement. Whitlock is a shining example of the power of using one's platform for good through his philanthropic endeavors, community involvement, and support for gymnastics and sports. In addition to his athletic prowess, his life story is one of kindness, generosity, and a resolve to improve the world. By considering his life and work as a whole, Whitlock has left an indelible mark that will encourage generations to come to achieve their full athletic and personal potential and to make positive changes in the world.

CHAPTER 12: FUTURE ENDEAVORS

A gymnast's career like Max Whitlock's is defined by outstanding accomplishments, dogged perseverance, and an unwavering resolve to succeed. His future is filled with endless possibilities as he moves on from his competitive career. Each one reflects his passion for gymnastics, sports, and making a positive difference in society. He plans to inspire, influence, and contribute to the world in his future endeavors, not merely because of what he will do, but because of how he will do it.

Whitlock has been quite forthcoming about his post-retirement plans, and his passion for gymnastics is clearly going to be a driving force. Continuing his involvement in the sport that has brought him so much joy is one of his main objectives. Coaching, mentoring, and even working in sports administration are all examples of ways in which one can get involved. When it comes to gymnastics, Whitlock is a priceless asset thanks to his knowledge, experience, and skill. As a gymnast who went from nowhere to become an Olympic champion, he has a special perspective that he can impart to young gymnasts. Whitlock can help guide the careers of aspiring athletes through the ups and downs by taking on the role of coach or mentor.

But technical abilities are just one part of coaching. A balanced lifestyle, mental toughness, and resilience are all parts of Whitlock's holistic approach to gymnastics that can help young athletes succeed. In order to mold athletes with exceptional physical ability and mental fortitude, his emphasis on mental health and wellness, informed by his personal experiences, will be pivotal. As a mentor, Whitlock is compassionate and helpful because he understands the difficulties of competing at a high level.

Whitlock is interested in sports administration as well as coaching. One of his goals for gymnastics's future is to ensure that all people are able to participate. Whitlock can promote these values by assuming a position in gymnastics administration and fighting for programs and policies that do just that. With his personal experience in the sport and understanding of the resources needed for athletes to succeed, he is in a prime position to bring about positive change in the gymnastics community. Whitlock's participation in administration can also assist with resolving concerns like funding, athlete welfare, and creating grassroots programs to guarantee a consistent supply of talent.

It is possible that Whitlock will investigate opportunities outside of gymnastics as part of his future pursuits. His previous endeavors, like the Max Whitlock Gymnastics Club, demonstrate his entrepreneurial spirit. Whitlock has an entrepreneurial spirit and could pursue many opportunities in the business world that are a good fit for his skills and interests. He has the potential to expand his brand and influence into new areas, such as health and wellness, fitness program development, or even gymnastics apparel.

Opportunities in broadcasting and the media present themselves to Whitlock as a result of his public image and media presence. Sports commentary or hosting would be a perfect fit for his charisma, knowledge of gymnastics, and eloquence. Whitlock can maintain his position as a prominent figure in gymnastics by continuing to educate and entertain audiences with his insights and analysis. He would be an asset to any media team thanks to his charisma and ability to simplify difficult concepts.

Whitlock will most certainly continue to devote a significant portion of his life after retirement to philanthropy and community service. A constant throughout his career has been and will continue to be his dedication to helping others and supporting charitable causes. Youth development, mental health, and sports accessibility initiatives can benefit from Whitlock's influence. He can keep making a difference in people's lives by forming partnerships with organizations and starting his own charitable projects. He is well-equipped to raise awareness and garner support for these causes thanks to his platform and life experiences.

Whitlock might also try to get people to live healthier lives and participate in sports. His experiences and successes make him an inspiration for those who want to spread the word about how good it is to be physically active and maintain a healthy lifestyle. Whitlock can promote fitness, mental health, and resilience through public speaking, workshops, and partnerships with health organizations. His goal is to encourage people of all ages to live better, more active lives by sharing his experience and the lessons he has learnt.

Even when Whitlock isn't physically present, he has an impact. The influence he has on digital and social media platforms puts him in front of people all over the world. He can keep interacting with his audience, offering advice, and speaking out for what he believes in through these platforms. His genuineness and ability to connect with his audience make his messages powerful and meaningful. He can engage and inspire his audience with digital content like fitness tutorials, motivational talks, and behind-the-scenes looks into his life.

Whitlock is leaving behind an extensive and varied legacy. The passion, perseverance, and relentless pursuit of perfection that have characterized his gymnastics career will surely inform his future pursuits. Whitlock will be greatly missed as he takes on new responsibilities, whether it's in gymnastics or elsewhere. His influence will be felt long after he retires from competitive gymnastics thanks to his contributions to the sport, his charitable endeavors, and his advocacy work.

Finally, there is much hope and promise for Max Whitlock's future. Various pursuits, including his love of gymnastics, his desire to start his own business, and his desire to make a difference, are in his plans for after retirement. Whitlock will always have a positive impact, whether through coaching, managing sports, running businesses, working in the media, or philanthropy. Hard work, perseverance, and a desire to make a difference are the driving forces behind his remarkable journey. The world will get to see Max Whitlock's incredible legacy continue in its next phase as he begins this new chapter.

CHAPTER 13: LEGACY AND IMPACT

Max Whitlock is a legendary figure in British gymnastics, a discipline he revolutionized with his boundless energy, unparalleled skill, and profound impact. His meteoric rise from young gymnast with promise to international superstar is a tribute to his relentless pursuit of greatness as well as his athletic ability. Whitlock has left an indelible mark on the sport of gymnastics, as well as on subsequent generations, and on British gymnastics in particular.

Whitlock has made significant contributions to the sport of British gymnastics. British gymnastics did not enjoy its current degree of worldwide renown prior to his ascent. The story was altered by Whitlock's revolutionary accomplishments. A new generation of British gymnasts has been inspired by his global success, which has put the sport in the national spotlight and elevated the profile of the sport. He has won multiple medals at the Olympics and World Championships.

His work in expanding the abilities of British gymnasts is one of Whitlock's most important contributions. Particularly on the pommel horse, his groundbreaking routines have revolutionized the sport. Whitlock has received praise and awe from all corners of the globe for his unfailing capacity to perform at a high level, flawlessly carrying out challenging routines. His unwavering commitment to honing his skills has not only paid dividends for himself, but has also served as an inspiration to his teammates and rivals.

Even after he has finished his competitive career, Whitlock has had an impact. Using his celebrity to spread the word about gymnastics and inspire people of all ages to get involved, he has been an outspoken supporter of the sport. By opening up about his love of gymnastics in interviews, public appearances, and on social media, Whitlock has helped bring the sport to a wider audience. His work has broken down barriers and made gymnastics more accessible, which has encouraged more young people to participate.

It is impossible to exaggerate the significance of Whitlock's impact on subsequent generations. His tenacity, perseverance, and commitment serve as an example for others to follow. The story of his journey is an inspiring one of overcoming obstacles, establishing objectives, and realizing aspirations via dogged persistence. Young gymnasts find encouragement and inspiration in Whitlock's story. It is feasible to reach the peak of one's sport with the correct attitude and persistence, as his accomplishments show.

One part of Whitlock's legacy that will endure is his dedication to community service. Young people now have access to top-notch coaching and facilities thanks to his programs like the Max Whitlock Gymnastics Club, which he founded to encourage participation in the sport. In addition to developing future gymnastics superstars, these programs aim to inspire a lifelong love of the sport and encourage kids and teens to get moving.

Besides his work with young gymnasts, Whitlock has been active in a number of community engagement and charitable projects. Causes like youth development, mental health awareness, and sports accessibility show his dedication to making a difference in the world. Whitlock has been able to leave an indelible mark as a positive force in society by using his position to promote causes that are close to his heart and those that share his beliefs.

One aspect of Whitlock's impact on British gymnastics is the way he helped shift public opinion. Because of his achievements, gender bias and other misconceptions about gymnastics have been disproven. Whitlock, a male gymnast, has proven that gender is irrelevant in the sport of gymnastics. As a result of his successes, more people are starting to support male gymnasts and the sport as a whole.

As a sport, British gymnastics continues to thrive thanks to Whitlock's legacies. Greater funding and support for gymnastics programs nationwide has resulted from the sport's elevated profile, which has been boosted by his accomplishments. As a result, the system for nurturing future gymnasts is stronger than before, guaranteeing that the sport will continue to thrive in the years to come.

Whitlock is also well-known on a global scale. In addition to raising the bar, his feats have aided in gymnastics' overall development. Gymnasts all over the world look up to him as an inspiration for pushing the sport to new heights with his daring routines and groundbreaking techniques. Whitlock inspired innovation and greatness in gymnastics and helped advance the sport.

Even after Whitlock retires from competitive gymnastics, his legacy will live on in the sport. He will continue to be an influential figure in the sport, whether it's through coaching, mentoring, or sports administration. Positive changes will be driven within the gymnastics community by his vision for the sport's future, which includes making it more accessible, inclusive, and supportive of athletes' well-being.

Finally, Max Whitlock left behind an impressive body of work that has had a profound and enduring effect on many fields. His accomplishments have revolutionized British gymnastics, paving the way for a fresh wave of talented gymnasts and taking the sport to unprecedented levels of success. Whitlock has permanently altered the trajectory of gymnastics via his perseverance, dedication, and involvement in the community. The medals he won are only a small part of his legacy; it also includes the motivation he gave, the records he broke, and the causes he championed for change. No matter what the future holds for gymnastics, Whitlock's impact will reverbcrate as he begins a new chapter in his life.

CONCLUSION

The story of Max Whitlock, a young gymnast with an unyielding will to succeed who went on to become an Olympic champion, is one of dogged determination, selfless service, and the life-altering impact of athletics. Max Whitlock's legacy lives on in the biography "MAX WHITLOCK: BEYOND THE GOLD - THE INSPIRING JOURNEY OF BRITAIN'S GYMNASTICS LEGEND," which details his incredible accomplishments and the lasting influence he had on the sport in Britain and beyond.

Whitlock started her rise to gymnastics stardom at a young age. The Hemel Hempstead, Hertfordshire, native Max showed an early talent for the art of gymnastics. He joined a neighborhood gymnastics club after his parents saw his promise; there, his aptitude and dedication to the sport became immediately apparent. Max refined his abilities with the help of his coaches, growing in strength and precision that would characterize his professional career.

He made little but noticeable strides forward in the early stages of his career. Whitlock started to gain recognition when he competed in both regional and national events. When he won silver in the all-around and gold in the team event at the 2010 Commonwealth Games in Delhi, he finally broke through. It was with this victory that British gymnastics welcomed a new star and laid the groundwork for his future greatness.

During the 2012 London Olympics, Max's career took a giant leap. The British men's gymnastics team, of which he was a key member, won a bronze medal—the country's first team medal in 100 years. This success marked a turning point in his career; it catapulted him into the limelight on a national level and cemented his place as an iconic figure in British gymnastics.

Whitlock's outstanding consistency and excellence propelled his career to new heights. For him, the highlight of his career came at the 2016 Olympics in Rio. Max made history as the first British gymnast to ever win an individual Olympic gold medal, with his victories in the pommel horse and floor exercises. Both fans and fellow athletes looked up to him because of how technically proficient and artistically executed his performances were.

Whitlock has had an enormous effect on British gymnastics, and it's not just because of her medals and accolades. Along with raising the bar for gymnastics, he has encouraged a new wave of young athletes to follow their passion. As a result of his achievements, gymnastics has received more attention than ever before, which has boosted both participation and funding for programs all over the United Kingdom. By going up against long-established dominance and demonstrating that Great Britain can produce world-class athletes, Whitlock has catapulted British gymnastics to the forefront of international attention.

Looking back on his career, it's easy to see that Whitlock had an impact well beyond his organ performances. His platform has allowed him to promote gymnastics and inspire young people to participate, and he has been an outspoken supporter of the sport. As an example of his dedication to community service, he volunteers with the Max Whitlock Gymnastics Club. He is making sure that gymnasts of the future have access to top-notch training and facilities by doing this.

An additional theme running through Whitlock's story is triumph over hardship. He has overcome many obstacles, such as injuries and fierce competition, throughout his career. Many have found motivation in his tenacity and resolve in the face of adversity. Max proved that it takes more than natural ability to achieve great things; it also requires self-control, dedication, and an insatiable thirst for success.

He has done much more for gymnastics than just perform and advocate for the sport. Whitlock has also contributed to the development of the game. Inspiring others to test their limits and set new standards, his groundbreaking routines and techniques have revolutionized gymnastics. His direct and indirect effects on gymnastics have shaped the sport around the world.

Much can be learned from Whitlock's story for generations to come. The significance of perseverance, commitment, and hard work is highlighted by his story. It demonstrates that surpassing one's limitations and maintaining a relentless work ethic are the keys to success. Max encourages aspiring gymnasts and athletes to maintain focus, welcome challenges, and persevere through dreams.

He leaves behind an impression and a legacy of inspiration. Not only has Max Whitlock accomplished much, but he has also set a precedent for other athletes to follow. He made an indelible mark on British gymnastics and on the sporting world at large with his contributions. The young gymnasts look up to him because he is a great example of honesty, dedication, and athleticism.

A story of enthusiasm, commitment, and influence emerges from Whitlock's life and work reflections. From his humble beginnings in Hemel Hempstead to his spectacular global achievements, Max's story exemplifies the power of determination and hard work. His outstanding skill and dedication to the sport are demonstrated by his numerous medals at the Olympic and World Championship levels.

The significance of Whitlock's contributions is further demonstrated by the honors and recognitions he has received. In recognition of his contributions to gymnastics, he was posthumously made an MBE and, subsequently, an OBE, among his many honours. His contributions to the sport and the community at large are recognized by these accolades, which go beyond his athletic accomplishments.

A simple but profound piece of advice from Whitlock to generations to come: have faith in yourself, work hard, and don't give up on your goals. His life exemplifies the power of perseverance and the promise that anything is achievable through hard work and commitment. Inspiring and motivating athletes for years to come, his legacy will ensure that his impact on the sport and the community endures.

Max Whitlock's journey and the accomplishments he has accomplished serve as a reminder of how sport can bring people together, change their perspectives, and ultimately change their lives. His legacy will reverberate with subsequent generations, and his story is an inspiration because it shows that we can all be great. To truly appreciate Max Whitlock's impact, we must do what he has done and more to spread the ideals he represents. Only then can we hope to see the next generation of athletes follow in his footsteps and give their all to their chosen fields.

Printed in Great Britain
by Amazon

54830927R00057